WRITE NOW

For Marisa Januzzi,
kindred spirit.

WRITE NOW

Harriet Griffey

**EXERCISES, PROMPTS & INSPIRATION
TO SPARK YOUR CREATIVE WRITING**

Hardie Grant

BOOKS

Contents

Getting Started	6
Voice	9
Narrative	17
Plot & Structure	29
Characterisation	37
Dialogue	47
Point of View	55
Place	67
Factual Writing	75
Fiction	85
Prose	93
Poetry	101
Memoir	117
What Next?	122
Further Reading	125

Getting Started

'Write every day. Don't ever stop. If you are unpublished, enjoy the act of writing – and if you are published, keep enjoying the act of writing. Don't become self-satisfied, don't stop moving ahead, growing, making it new. The stakes are high. Why else would we write?'

RICK BASS, AMERICAN WRITER, NOVELIST AND AUTHOR OF SHORT STORY COLLECTION *FOR A LITTLE WHILE*

Whether you've only ever written a shopping list or a work email, or thousands of words in your head but never on paper, writing is always the manifestation of some form of storytelling and, at its simplest, that's what writers do. They create stories, whether in fact or fiction, and this is one of the ways we organise our thoughts, respond to and make sense of the world in which we live. The earliest stories, nursery rhymes and fairy stories heard as a child all help the process of working out what we think and feel about our lives, our friends, ourselves.

In his book about children's fairy tales called *The Uses of Enchantment*, psychoanalyst Bruno Bettelheim wrote, 'Each fairy tale is a magic mirror which reflects some aspects of our inner world, and of the steps required by our evolution from immaturity to maturity.'

Whatever writing you want to do – poetry or prose, fact or fiction – it will afford you the opportunity to enhance your confidence and expertise in using words to good effect, to make your thoughts coherent and to develop self-expression, all in an individual way. This book is designed to help you establish your own writing practice, through a series of prompts that you can follow or dip into, consecutively or otherwise, depending on what you wish to focus on in terms of developing your writing.

And however creative you are, you still have to craft and wield those words and find your own 'voice'. This writing voice is one which feels true to you and recognisably *you* to others, which can adapt and accommodate whatever form you choose to write in, and in which you feel confident that you can work and explore your own ideas.

For Anne Frank, her daily journal was exactly this, about which she said: 'I want to write, but more than that, I want to bring out all kinds of things that lie buried deep in my heart.' And while you don't need to write every day, it's good to keep a notebook or journal in between and alongside writing projects, helping you develop confidence in your own work.

William Zinsser, American writer, editor and author of *On Writing Well*, said: 'You learn to write by writing.' There is no way around this. If you want to write, you have to get on and do it. For some, this is a burning *raison d'être* and for others it's a slog, but write they do and in the writing some alchemy of thoughts and words emerges on the page.

01

Voice

If you are serious about your writing, then you will know that finding your voice is an important part of your development as a writer. Voice comes from the process of writing because it's also linked to your confidence as a writer, which increases over time and through practice. It's a personal blueprint, even if we adjust it to what we're saying as much as we might our speaking voice. But first and foremost, our voice has to be an expression of our authentic selves.

Developing your writer's voice takes time and only becomes comfortable through use and exploration. That initial exploration can come about through copying others, which is common, so expect some false starts, which often feel like poor replicas and come across initially as derivative. But it's all useful practice and particularly valuable to finding a voice in which to write, homing in on what feels right.

EXERCISE 1

Think about how you would describe, to a friend, a series of events in your day: for example, a bus journey, a meal, a walk through the park. It doesn't matter what it is but it gives you some material with which to engage and which you can make engaging to someone else, through your storytelling. Irrespective of your age or gender, try the following, bearing in mind the context of that experience physically and mentally, the vocabulary you might use, the structure of the sentence, the preoccupations that might run alongside your experience of whichever event you are recounting. Let your imagination fly, but keep in character and aim for consistency in the voice you use.

- First tell the story in the voice of a young girl, 100 years ago.
- Second, recount the same event in the voice of an elderly man, today.
- Now, tell the exact same story as yourself, pitching your voice against those previously used, making it as authentically you as you can. The purpose of the first two efforts is to help clarify a sense of yourself, in contrast to others.

This exercise is to help you gain confidence in your own voice, before you develop it across whichever form of writing you want, adapting it but keeping it true to you.

EXERCISE 2

Take a look at what you've written. In particular, look at the adjectives you've used. How accurately do these reflect the sort of vocabulary you'd use in real life? How can you expand on this? Compare this with how you'd speak to a friend and see how far, on paper, your writing voice reflects the way you'd tell a story in person. Rather than be 'writerly' about it, be authentic. Remember, this is the practice that will help you discover a comfortable, confident voice in which to work.

EXERCISE 3

Choose something with which you're really familiar — an event, a meeting with someone, or an object that's important to you. Then taking these two writers as examples, write:

- First, one long, heavily punctuated sentence, like Proust.

"That year, when my parents had decided which day we would be returning to Paris, a little earlier than usual, on the morning of our departure, after they had my hair curled for a photograph, and carefully placed on my head a hat I had never worn before and dressed me in a quilted velvet coat, after looking for me everywhere, my mother found me in tears on the steep little path beside Tansonville, saying good-bye to the hawthorns, putting my arms around the prickly branches, and, like the princess in the tragedy burdened by vain ornaments, ungrateful to the importunate hand that with such care had gathered my hair in curls across my brow, trampling underfoot my torn-out curl papers and my new hat."

FROM *IN SEARCH OF LOST TIME*, VOLUME 1, TRS. LYDIA DAVIS

- Second, nine short ones like Hemingway, writing about whatever you've chosen.

"Now is not the time to think of baseball, he thought. Now is the time to think of only one thing. That which I was born for. There might be a big one around that school, he thought. I picked up only a straggler from the albacore that were feeding. But they are working far out and fast. Everything that shows on the surface travels very fast and to the north-east. Can that be the time of day? Or is it some sign of weather that I do not know?"

FROM *THE OLD MAN AND THE SEA*

- Now, in your own words, and in your own voice, write a similar length paragraph about the same thing.

EXERCISE 4

It's easier to find your voice when writing about things you actively care about. Jotting down the subject of your enthusiasm or concern, along with a note of those words that resonate with, reflect on or reference it, starts to create the blueprint from which to explore an authentic voice. For example, you may be passionate about 18th-century samplers, so your notes may include references to fabric, threads, colours, textures, the content of a sampler and the nature of the work, painstaking and precise.

EXERCISE 5

What does the word *voice* mean to you? How would you describe different voices? Make a list of at least 12 different characteristics of voice, from the idea that 'Her voice was ever soft, gentle and low; an excellent thing in a woman' (as King Lear describes his daughter, Cordelia's voice, in Shakespeare's eponymous play) to that of a fishwife, or child or old man. Now describe your own. This will help you think about what supports or differentiates the qualities of one voice from another.

Things To Remember

- Read. This is going to come up time and time again, but unless you read different examples of voice, you won't have a range of contexts against which to pitch and discover your own.

- Don't get hung up on perfection: every effort is perfect, because it brings you closer to feeling what's right.

- Practice is necessary, and this is the writing that no one will ever see.

02

Narrative

Narrative is an account of a series of events that, when linked together, tell a story. That story can be in fictional prose or poetry form or, in the case of a news or historical narrative, non-fiction. Narrative doesn't necessarily need a narrator, but the writer's job is to tell the story in one form or another and via a particular point of view, which can influence how the narrative is told. For example, if it's a crime novel told from the point of view of the detective, then the narrative will be limited to what he or she discovers, as it is discovered. This creates tension and will also have an influence on how the narrative is plotted.

Narrative is also linked to cause and effect; because *this* happened, then *that* happened. There has to be a reason — even if this isn't immediately revealed, or revealed retrospectively — why the elements of a story are being told. Even if a story is made up, it must feel plausible and, given that truth is often stranger than fiction, there's a lot of leeway for an active imagination.

EXERCISE 6

Even the simplest fairy story of Cinderella has a distinct and satisfying narrative: the fairy godmother saves the day, step-sisters get their come-uppance, good triumphs over evil, and Cinderella – finally – gets her prince. This is an example of a narrative statement. Using this basic narrative, write a comparable fairy tale that subverts some of its components to give it a modern twist.

EXERCISE 7

Take a piece of your own writing – this can even be a short exploratory piece of journal writing – to identify what you feel is your narrative statement in that instance. Alternatively, take a couple of your favourite books, fiction or non-fiction, and identify what you feel to be their narrative statements.

EXERCISE 8

Starting with the words 'Once upon a time...' see how you can use time in a piece of writing, but not chronologically. Make your use of time nonlinear, so the narrative doesn't progress smoothly through time but moves backwards and forwards either through the action, or the main character's thoughts or memories.

EXERCISE 9

Biography   Memoir
Captivity narrative   Nonlinear narrative
Fantasy   Quest narrative
Historical fiction   Short story

For each of the eight categories of narrative form listed above, identify an example of each. Now take one of the narrative forms and map out a storyline that is appropriate to it.

EXERCISE 10

Molly Bloom's soliloquy in James Joyce's *Ulysses* deliberately lacks punctuation and grammar, and this shows us the way in which her thoughts range across different ideas without restriction. In a similar way, compose 500 words either of your own thoughts or those of a fictional character (it's probably easier to go with your own thoughts first) in an effort to get that freedom of narrative style and voice which suggests an interior monologue. This may help you in the development of a specific character's voice, or a writing voice of your own.

EXERCISE 11

There are numerous narrative devices available to writers that can help create mood, tension and excitement to vary the pace of the narrative and engage the reader. These include the use of sentence length, flashbacks, interior thoughts, foreshadowing, pathetic fallacy, dramatic irony, metaphor and personification. Take a previous piece of writing and consider what you could do to rewrite it in a way that makes it a more vivid piece, using some of the devices listed above.

EXERCISE 12

Sustaining your writing across a narrative is often helped by working out how you might progress it. Where will you start? Start with your exposition. Then consider what information you might withhold for later effect. Mapping out a sequence of events, drawn perhaps from a personal experience, can be a first step in imagining different ways of constructing a narrative.

EXERCISE 13

On any journey – which always has a beginning, middle and an end – consider by whom a narrative of a journey might be told. For what purpose is the journey made? Through whose eyes is it explored? Is it told in linear fashion, as it happened, or in flashback? Draft 500 words that map out the beginning, middle and end, then see what you have to work with.

EXERCISE 14

Unless you are clear about who the main protagonist is, it can be difficult to write a convincing narrative. Sometimes it is obvious, sometimes not: clarify this in your own mind by detailing bullet points of narrative and see which bits are linked to which characters, in order for the story to be told.

EXERCISE 15

Free associate – allow your mind to make interesting connections between information and facts – and jot down a personal narrative: some family story that is often repeated. Then consider it from a point of view other than your own.

EXERCISE 16

What does the word story mean to you? Explore its personal connotations and make notes, as well as writing down alternative words for story, such as fable or myth. Free associate and jot down whatever comes to mind, all of which can help refresh your approach when it comes to storytelling.

Things To Remember

- Whatever narrative form you have chosen, keep it consistent.

- Ensure you are clear on the narrative point: make a note of it.

- Be clear on your main protagonist, whether writing fiction or fact.

- Edit and re-edit: focus on what tells the story and remove anything that is superfluous to its narrative.

03
Plot & Structure

If a narrative is structured by a sequence of events, it is how those events come together, answering all the whys, the wherefores, the hows, and the whens of the whos, that constitutes its plot. How the action is plotted in order to tell that story is done through the imagination, skill and craft of the writer.

Some novelists plot to within an inch of their lives, sequencing the whole trajectory of their work's action, with each event, scene or interaction carefully worked out. Others may have a sense of this in their head, and know where they might end up, but are happy to work out how they are going to get there as they go along. There is no 'right' way, but there are ground rules.

For instance, you may use a simple three-act plot (the beginning, middle, end) for your story, even if you don't use it in this sequence. Or you may employ, as is common in drama, a five-act plot, which can be useful to you as you write as it helps you see how to move the story along, keeping the reader engaged.

EXERCISE 17

Exposition *(the set-up)*
Rising action *(what happens)*
Climax *(pivotal point of change)*
Falling action *(what happens next)*
Denouement *(how things resolve)*

Take your idea and using the structure of the five-act plot (above), detail briefly what happens at each point. Once you have this template of a structure and know where you want to end up, you can play with the content to make it happen.

EXERCISE 18

Protagonist/antagonist
Desire/want/need
Journey/overcoming of obstacles
Climax/crisis
Resolution

Sequence your own story (fictional or personal), or that of a well-loved novel, so you can identify how it breaks down into the five component parts of storytelling outlined above. Identifying these and keeping them in mind will create a template with which you can work.

EXERCISE 19

'It was dark inside the wolf.'
MARGARET ATWOOD'S PROPOSED FIRST LINE IN THE RETELLING OF LITTLE RED RIDING HOOD.

Taking Atwood's suggestion, think of a basic and very familiar storyline, perhaps from a child's fairy tale, and in note form, reimagine the plot of that story to give a new structure to its narrative.

EXERCISE 20

Identify the *point* of your story and sum it up in no more than 20 words. This is similar to an 'elevator pitch' and it's key: if you aren't clear on the point of the story you're telling when you start, it will be hard to stay on track throughout the writing of it. From this, everything else can evolve.

EXERCISE 21

Consider this six-word story attributed to Ernest Hemingway: 'For sale: baby shoes. Never worn.' From this you can extrapolate myriad reasons about why the shoes were never worn, the context and the characters; but everything you could imagine and write as a consequence of stringing these six words together is the result of some event. Write your own six-word story.

EXERCISE 22

What do you like in a plot? What are your expectations? Describe the demands you, as a reader, make: do you want to be immersed, provoked, amused by what you read? Think about your favourite books and identify what engaged you and made that book successful for you. Write it all down. This is just one reader, you, but it will make you focus on what you need to achieve as a writer, to please your inner critic.

EXERCISE 23

Take the word plot. Think about its various meanings. Explore some of its many associations from the idea of a patch of ground, and what might grow in or arise from it, to the idea of plot as conspiracy. Make a list of a minimum of 12 words that are all related to things you associate with the word plot. This will help your vocabulary, but it will also make interesting connections that can help you imagine how to create a compelling plot for your writing.

Things To Remember

- Be clear on the point of the story. It is a useful reference to return to time and time again, even if how you tell your story changes.

- Know where you want to get to, even if the immediate sequence of events still need to be worked out.

- Mapping out the key elements of structure and how they might be sequenced to maximum effect is a useful exercise.

- Be flexible: allow for development and structural shifts as the story gets told.

04

Characterisation

Creating characters that feel real, whom readers can engage with and believe in, lies at the heart of great storytelling. When you consider some of the most memorable fictional personalities — sometimes not always likeable — there will always be some hook that makes a story's protagonist relatable, whether that's Jane Eyre or Eleanor Oliphant, Alexander Portnoy or Harry Potter. Writers can't necessarily second guess what that point of empathy will be for a reader, but in a multi-dimensional character there will be traits with which readers can identify and empathise.

For all characters, but especially the main protagonist, the writer must know all about them, even if they only divulge those aspects of their character that are relevant. Even if what is used in the telling of their story is the tip of an iceberg of information, the writer's knowledge of their character will inform how they respond or react, their thoughts and actions, what they say (or don't) and how they say it. Writers need to know their characters inside out, while always allowing room for that human characteristic of unpredictability, within what the writer knows of their character and the circumstances of their story.

EXERCISE 24

For any fictional character, write down their full name, date of birth, where they were born, parents (known, unknown, dead or alive), sibling relationships (or not), what they look like, any quirky features or physical characteristics, interests and so on, so that you have the sense of a fully rounded character — even if you never reveal any of this in the writing because it's not explicitly relevant. This is what will underpin your writing of a character and it's similar to what actors do when they inhabit a role. They know the back story. It keeps you on track if there's a specificity to your knowledge and this will help inform how the relationships between characters pan out, too.

EXERCISE 25

Now take it a little further and pinpoint some minor details that will flesh out a character: remember, an author may never use these details in the writing, but it fixes the character in *their* mind's eye and will lend coherence to the writing. For example:

- What's their favourite food?
- How is their hair styled?
- What shoes do they wear?

EXERCISE 26

Choosing names for your characters is an important facet of your role as a writer, as all names come with associative links. These might be historical or class related, and you can see how this works for you in the following exercise.

For each of the names listed below, draft a short character sketch that links the associations you make to the name:

Meredith	Horatio	Brooklyn
Olive	Jasper	Lordes
Mackenzie	Bob	Caitlin

EXERCISE 27

Take six famous literary characters, or six of your own, and sum each of them up in six words.

EXERCISE 28

Draft a character whose personality appears to be flawed, someone unlikeable but relatable. A complete antihero, if you like. Complete the exercise by identifying the five key words you feel sum them up.

EXERCISE 29

In casting the characters for your story, find the protagonist first and then sketch out what other characters will be necessary to the plot to tell the story.

EXERCISE 30

In creating characters, consider providing details about them:

- Through what other characters say;
- Through an exchange of dialogue;
- Through their actions;
- Through their thoughts;

Write one line of description about a character. Using this description, write another line as if someone else were describing that character. Now create a line or two of dialogue that demonstrates the same. Again, using your first description, how might this characteristic be demonstrated through action? Finally, in reflection, how might these characteristics appear through the character's thoughts?

EXERCISE 31

Take a very ordinary, mundane, everyday event like doing the washing up and describe it through a character's actions, their body language, what they might say or do while doing it – and what they don't. Don't resort to adverbs, either: saying he or she walked carefully isn't good enough. Say, instead, something like he or she walked as if their shoes were soaked.

EXERCISE 32

Make short character sketches from what you observe of people you don't know; fellow travellers on a bus, people in a cinema queue, those at a supermarket checkout. Maybe it's something they're wearing, an accent or turn of phrase they've used, a physical gesture: something that for you says 'character', something specific that caught your eye and that you feel could be characteristic of them.

EXERCISE 33

Select a sample of friends or family members and make a list of key words that you feel sum up their character — you can include yourself here, too. Now take each adjective and develop it, consider similes and metaphors, check for specificity — how accurate a term is this for what you want to describe about that person? For example, if someone is by nature a calm person, how else might that characteristic be described?

Things To Remember

- Characters don't need to be over-described: allow the reader space to bring their own reactions to bear.

- Depending on the story's structure or plot, a slow reveal can allow readers the space to react.

- Ambiguity and unreliability might be useful ways to use characters.

- Some basic facts always need to remain consistent; if their eyes are blue, they stay blue.

- We also learn about other people through what we are told, what we see and what we hear. Use second person narratives as opportunities for character development.

05

Dialogue

In real life, people exchange incomplete sentences, inconsequential half-thoughts and inanities. They interrupt and talk over each other, using clichés and mixed metaphors and inaccurate or profane vocabulary. Real people say 'um' and 'er' and 'well' and 'anyway' *a lot*, which would look ridiculous if realistically peppered through written dialogue. Within those more mundane and meandering conversations of real life are nuggets of consequence, and it is these that need to be utilised in written dialogue. What a writer needs to do is isolate these nuggets, and then find the sound and rhythm of what needs saying, and have their character say it.

Dialogue in fiction isn't real but a semblance of reality, a representation of spoken exchanges. Dialogue has to be explicit to the story: we don't hear conversations that don't matter to the narrative. What it is that matters might be a specific fact, or an impression or a misunderstanding, but it's something that will drive the plot forward in some way. Dialogue also enables a writer to convey characters' personalities through the way that they speak, through what they say and what they don't, especially if they are withholding key information.

EXERCISE 34

Imagine two young people in conversation, one telling the other about a great night out they've had – the details of this are up to you. Through the dialogue it should be apparent – partly in what's *not* said – that these two know each other well. And it should be clear what sort of young people they are too, perhaps through their choice of vocabulary or turn of phrase.

EXERCISE 35

One of the good reasons for writers to carry a notebook at all times is to be able to record snippets of conversation that are unique. If you are observing strangers, it's also possible to glean information not only from what they say in conversation, but also how they say it. Make a note of your observations about body language and other details, too.

EXERCISE 36

The vocabulary used in dialogue will provide an immediate link to its speaker through the choice of words. Bearing this in mind, draft a line of dialogue depicting how four different characters – a child of six, a teenage boy, a young woman in her 20s, a man in his 60s – would describe a meal they'd really enjoyed, that makes it immediately obvious which character is which.

EXERCISE 37

In order to move the plot forward, combine the plot's action with dialogue. Draft an exchange that does this between, for example, an estranged couple meeting again by accident, without repeating in dialogue something covered by a description of what they are doing, thinking or feeling and vice versa.

EXERCISE 38

Capture fragments of real-life conversations when you can. Select a few choice phrases and then riff on these, imagining the lives of the people who've spoken them. Create personalities and flesh out their characters, using the clues given by what they said and how they said it, along with your observations of them.

EXERCISE 39

Identify a few potential characters and list different word choices that might be a reflection of their age, ethnicity, education, location and circumstances. Avoid stereotypes and look for more subtle variations, trying to be as authentic as possible.

Things To Remember

- Concern yourself with <u>what</u> your characters say, first, before you refine <u>how</u> they say it.
- Speech should *sound* realistic; it doesn't have to be real.
- Dialogue should help drive the plot, not hinder it.
- Writing dialogue takes practice in order to get a character's voice *right*.
- Expect to play with dialogue to get it a) right and b) in the right place.

06

Point of View

The point of view in a piece of writing, and how this is expressed, is linked to your choice of narration and whether it is written in the first person, second or third. A narrator can have various manifestations, including being the main character, an observer, maybe a child's eye view, an omniscient or an unreliable narrator. There are all sorts of ways to vary how a story is told through the choice of a specific point of view. What is crucial is that having selected a point of view from which to write, it must be consistent. Without consistency the writing loses credibility and along with that it will lose the confidence of its reader.

EXERCISE 40

First-person narrator
USES 'I'

This uses first-person pronouns I, we, us, and is a very straightforward way of telling a story, although it means you have to inhabit that character. If this is not your actual self, you're going to have to be very clear and consistent about who that person is, what you have them know and don't know, as the story is written. You can't know, for example, what's going on inside anyone else's head, only your own character's from their point of view; every opinion expressed is that of this character's and the story can only be told from their viewpoint.

Write about walking into an event where you see someone that you've not seen in years and with whom you share a difficult secret. The circumstances and what you feel about this person is up to your character.

EXERCISE 41

Second-person narrator
USES 'YOU'

Second-person narration is often used in non-fiction writing like self-help books or instruction manuals and even cookery books. It feels instructive because it addresses and suggests to a reader what they should or ought to do. It's less commonly used in fiction, because although it enhances a reader's involvement it can also feel almost as if the voice in the story is the voice in our own heads, and as if it is our own experience as much as that of the story's character. For emotionally driven stories, this can have a powerful effect. Usually also written in the present tense, this point of view also promotes a sense of immediacy and intimacy.

Using the second-person and present tense form, write about something, an experience (perhaps one you've had) or event, which creates, for example, a sense of fear, whether this is something like riding on a rollercoaster or being abducted at gunpoint. Start with the words, 'You need to understand that it wasn't something you would want to do...' and take it from there.

EXERCISE 42

Third-person narrator
USES 'HE' OR 'SHE'

Perhaps the narrator we are most used to, especially in fiction. The implication is that it is the author who is the narrator of the story, even if this isn't the case in reality. The narrator is ostensibly an objective observer, someone who has access to all the facts, and is able to describe the thoughts, intentions and actions of a cast of characters, including their reported speech. This makes the narrator all-seeing, which cannot be true in real life but serves the telling of the story. Sometimes, however, the narrator isn't completely omniscient but limited to those actions, thoughts and ideas of only one character, and this can serve the story in a different way.

Start with a third-person limited point of view: you only have access to one character's thoughts, feelings and actions and there is no access to those of any other character – much like in real life. Having established who your narrator is, take an historical event (perhaps something about which you have either knowledge or personal experience) and write it up as fiction.

Now take the same piece of writing and rewrite it, changing it to a third-person omniscient point of view, one which allows you to include the thoughts, feelings and actions of other characters in your piece of writing.

EXERCISE 43

If you want to write from a child's point of view, it's important to understand the limitations of their understanding. However precocious you might want a child's eye view to be, there are aspects of life experience that can't yet be understood, for example, the nuances of adults' sexual behaviour. If you are using a child's viewpoint in order to tell a story, it must be consistent with a child's level of experience and understanding to ring true.

EXERCISE 44

Unreliable narrator

The definition of an unreliable narrator originates from a 1961 publication, *The Rhetoric of Fiction* by Wayne C. Booth. It's also easy to see its use in, for example, *The Girl on the Train* by Paula Hawkins, not least because the central character Rachel is a drunk, her narration made unreliable through alcohol and her delusional state, all of which is key to the story. Iain Banks' *The Wasp Factory* is about a dysfunctional family, whose dysfunction lies at the heart of the story, making its narration unreliable. In these cases, unreliable narration is a deliberate feature of the storytelling. Whether or not it's clear from the start if the narrator is unreliable or not is up to the writer, but as a feature in the story's drama it can create tension, keeping the reader guessing and adding unexpected twists in the story.

Write a passage about going to a shop to buy bread. How could you make your description of this simple act of purchase *feel* unreliable to a reader? How might what you write create *doubt* about what happened in the reader's mind? Think about the situation in which you place the event, the character profiles of those involved, the narrator's point of view, the location of the action: all the circumstances that could be brought into play in an unreliable or ambiguous way in order to recount this simple event.

EXERCISE 45

Multiple narrators

This can produce some interesting storytelling, particularly as it raises questions about the reliability of what the reader is told, depending on the narrator's point of view (or narrators' points of view). For example, in Emily Brontë's *Wuthering Heights*, the principal narrator of the story of Heathcliff and Catherine Earnshaw is Lockwood, but his narration is partly informed by that of Ellen 'Nelly' Dean who, as she says, tells the story 'in true gossip's fashion'. What the reader gets then is Nelly's version of events, but told through Lockwood's perspective, and further complicated by her speculation or what she understands from what someone else has told her.

Take any current news story, local, national or international, and consider not the main person's point of view, but that of a subsidiary character. Draft 500 words about how those same facts affected them and how they might tell that same story.

EXERCISE 46

Where narrator meets voice

Sometimes the choice of narration in a story is also coloured by the voice in which it's expressed. There's a use of a vernacular (the language or dialect spoken), idiom or cadence that's linked directly to the character speaking, which we see in novels where first-person voice has been used, like Toni Morrison's *Beloved*, Sebastian Barry's *Days Without End*, Margaret Atwood's *Alias Grace* and Mark Twain's *Huckleberry Finn*. Sometimes it serves to create a sense of where a character has originated from, their level of education or historical context. It works to add something specific to the storytelling through its use.

Without parody, but in the voice of someone whose native language is different from that in which they are trying to speak, describe a visit to a park using only diction (choice of words) and syntax (sentence structure) to convey the language difference.

EXERCISE 47

Imagine how some aspect of your own life – a first day at school or work, for example – might be remembered and recounted by someone else, perhaps someone who knows you well (a family member). Alternatively, you could imagine it told by someone whose observations are not coloured by personal knowledge of you, someone who had only just met you on that day.

EXERCISE 48

List some synonyms (words that mean the same thing) for the word *narration* and play with how they might change the nuance or emphasis of what you want to write.

Things To Remember

- Whichever point of view you choose, it must be consistent.

- Make sure you're clear about both the potential and the limitations of your choice, which will help you remain consistent.

- If you want to use a form of narration that relies on a particular way in which a character uses language, either in thought or spoken word, you have to stick with this voice throughout.

07

Place

The setting, the location or place in which writing is set can be given a life and language of its own, interacting with and influencing what happens in other aspects of the story. For example, Tolkien's Middle Earth in *The Lord of the Rings*, the sea in *Moby Dick*, the moors in *Wuthering Heights* and the fog in Charles Dickens' London as depicted in *Bleak House*.

The place, its location, geography and weather, can all be brought to bear to add colour or context, or to be used in some way to progress the plot. These are the circumstances in which people and situations exist and in some cases they can become a feature in their own right rather than just a mere backdrop to the action.

EXERCISE 49

Place

Consider one of the most famous opening lines in contemporary literature, from Daphne du Maurier's novel *Rebecca*: 'Last night I dreamt I went to Manderley again.' The house, to which the unnamed narrator returns to live after her marriage to its owner, Maxim de Winter, is an important part of this psychological thriller. The mysterious Gothic mansion on a cliff top in Cornwall contains and hides secrets, there are labyrinthine corridors, dark staircases, closed doors, mullioned windows and a minstrels' gallery. It would be hard to imagine the story *without* the brooding house, almost a reflection of the sense of malevolence surrounding the narrator.

Imagine a building or specific place, perhaps based on somewhere you know, and give it characteristics that could resonate with a possible theme of a story. What might it represent in this story?

EXERCISE 50

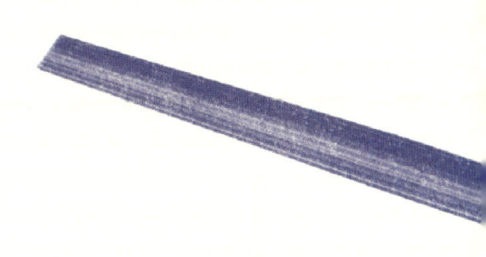

Geographical landscape

In another of her novels, *Jamaica Inn*, du Maurier utilises the isolated moorlands, wild seascape and harsh coastline of Cornwall even further in her tale of Mary Yellan, doing so not only for their drama but also as a way of reflecting the personality of her characters. We see this also in *The Waves* by Virginia Woolf, where the way the characters are written reflects the way waves crash over each other. Sometimes a location or aspect of place becomes almost as resonant as one of the actual characters; sometimes it can almost be the protagonist of the plot.

Consider a geographical area – moors, deserts, mountains, fenlands, prairies, forests, lakes – and describe it in terms of its features, as if writing a geography essay. Be specific and detailed. Look at pictures – or out of the window – and experience it in whatever way you can. Research it and, without cliché, write a straightforwardly descriptive piece. Then imagine whose story might evolve from such a landscape.

EXERCISE 51

Weather

Weather can be just a backdrop, a statement of fact that adds colour to a scene, or it can create atmosphere, reflect emotions, add tension and pathos and even be responsible for the course of a plot – think of Virginia Woolf's *To the Lighthouse,* in which a whole storyline is premised on a small boy's desire to go to the lighthouse and the trip being dependent on whether or not the weather is good enough.

While weather can be part of the setting, or symbolic of some kind of internal strife, it can also be used to create reasons for story elements. For example, what if it hadn't rained that day? Describe a scene where the impact of the weather changes the course of events. Consider how or why this might be.

EXERCISE 52

Think of a journey taken – anything from a first trip on a bus or plane, to walking the dog – and how that might be described and written in order to incorporate some internal journey for a character.

EXERCISE 53

Pathetic fallacy

Its original usage, as coined by John Ruskin, was to mean false feelings — which is the attribution of human moods, traits and feelings to the weather or inanimate objects. For example, 'the sullen rocks', 'the exuberant clouds' or 'the clock struck gloomily'. Shakespeare used pathetic fallacy in *King Lear*, in which the violent storm on the heath reflects the aged king's descent into madness, and elsewhere. It can be used to create interesting ways of expressing ideas in our prose that will evoke feelings and reactions in the reader. The trick to using pathetic fallacy is to avoid clichés and find new and original ways to use it in our writing to enhance atmosphere and suggest mood.

> 'When he got up the next morning, he boiled the kettle to make his tea, after which he took his cup to the garden to watch the dawn break.'

Rewrite the sentence above using the same words but with additions that attribute emotion to inanimate objects and the weather to suggest three different moods:

- He was sad.
- He was nervous.
- He was excited.

EXERCISE 54

As an exercise in observation, write in detail about today's weather, the temperature, quality of light, effect on what you hear, even its smell: make the description sensual. Now write about the memories this conjures up, or the way the weather makes you feel.

EXERCISE 55

Weather can be described in all sorts of ways. Make a list of alternative words and synonyms, turns of phrase (both hackneyed and original) for the following:

Stormy   Foggy   Windy
Hot   Wet   Mild

Things To Remember

- You can use place, location, geography and weather to simply set the scene or as an integral part of the story.

- Or, use these aspects to further the reader's experience through the way they depict emotions or feelings.

- How might a location affect the mood of its inhabitants? Midtown Manhattan is a very different experience to the mudflats of Suncheon Bay, Korea, for example.

- Avoid clichés or idiomatic language when describing the weather: saying it's raining cats and dogs won't work in historical fiction, for example.

08
Factual Writing

Creative writing can be both fiction *and* factual, using the same basic narrative tools to communicate ideas and information to a reader. But the assumption that the reader makes, and to which the writer adheres, is that factual writing is not made up. And that it isn't, to coin a phrase, 'fake news' but rooted in truthful fact.

Factual writing covers many forms: journalism, essays (academic or otherwise), blogging, non-fiction books covering everything from biography to cookery, it all requires a degree of knowledge, research and application in order to bring it into existence. It may include direct quotes or opinions, recount others' ideas or interpret events, but it is assumed to be non-fiction. It's also creative writing because the writer still has to create a narrative that keeps readers interested.

Also, because factual writing often requires accurate research, its practice can help enhance creative fiction writing, too. Interviewing people, and finding a way to express their voices, is great practice for honing both character and dialogue in fiction. If this is part of your daily writing practice, be reassured that it will a) help you find your own voice and b) give you the confidence to write anything you want. The research at the heart of a novel is the scaffold on which the fiction rests.

EXERCISE 56

News item

Who, what, where, when, why (and sometimes how)? These are the five questions that news stories have to answer. Typically, a news piece is around 400 words long, written in the third person, past tense, delivering the facts without much embellishment and with no personal opinions or subjective descriptions, although these may appear in reported speech or quotes. The most important line is the first line, which should contain all the essential facts, then a broader description follows. For example: When France beat Croatia 4-2 at the Luzhniki Stadium in Moscow on 15 July 2018, it was the first FIFA World Cup final to use the video assistant referee (VAR) system.

Scan today's news either online or in print, find an extended news story and then cut it to 400 words, making sure that the opening line or 'stand first' gives the full gist of the story in the simplest way.

EXERCISE 57

Feature writing

Longer features are often extended news items, sometimes with a more personal slant, and are often adjuncts to news stories. So, if there has been a news item on, say, a mental health issue, then a complementary feature might enlarge on or extend the news story. Sometimes it will be a first-person article, recounting a personal experience that complements the news item.

For feature writing, put together a three-line pitch, outlining a proposed, 1200-word feature that links to and enhances a news item.

EXERCISE 58

Long-form journalism
This is the closest form of journalism to an essay. Often commissioned to a specific brief, this may require research, interviewing and also structuring the piece in a way that reveals the story's core in a different way.

Long-form journalism requires a slightly longer pitch that could include details of interviewees specific to the piece. The 'who, what, where, when, why' approach can be applied here, too. Who, for example, would you interview, and why?

EXERCISE 59

Practise interviewing – with a recording device, so you can glean accurate quotes – by interviewing a family member, and start by focusing on something specific. For example, an older relative or friend may have a wealth of stories, but asking general questions such as, 'What was it like …' are difficult to answer. Better to say, 'Tell me about your first day at school, college, or work …' Prepare six questions beforehand, listen closely as your next question may come from what they've told you, and keep your recording device on throughout. Aim for 800–1,200 words of written interview with first-person quotes.

EXERCISE 60

Essay writing

The essay can be considered similar to long-form journalism, reportage and memoir and can be anything from 500 to 5,000 words in length. And while opinion lies at the heart of the essay, it requires more than that to explain ideas of personal, political or philosophical interest. Ideas are backed up by information and evidence, often taking the reader from the personal to the universal.

Writing an academic essay, with which many students and graduates are familiar, is a complementary but slightly different skill, by necessity showing evidence of successful learning and original thought. Well-structured, good prose writing is also essential.

What do you feel passionately about? This might be keeping hens, compiling music playlists, 19th-century women's basketball or the paintings of Piero della Francesca; it doesn't matter, but choose a subject about which you know something and would like to know more, then research and write an 800-word essay.

EXERCISE 61

Blogs

A blog — a contraction of 'web-log' — published online can be a really good place to explore, develop and publish writing. It can focus on a very specific subject or be a wide-ranging journal, it could be personal or more generic (and sometimes a platform for fictional writing). Content published in a blog can also be used to link to other websites, and networked across other platforms, X, Facebook and Instagram, for example, to build online traffic for your writing. Blogs are traditionally quite short, focused reads, written and published online regularly. Stumbling across a well-written blog, whose author is engaged in some exploration of a particular passion or preoccupation, can be both informative and entertaining.

With internet access, there's no reason not to set up a personal blog and create the discipline of writing regularly. Conforming to the standards of well-written prose still applies, so always aim for well-structured and well-edited content before you hit publish.

As your subject, take something in which you have some expertise, and write about it in a factual, informative but entertaining way. This might be dog grooming, Zumba dancing, 19-th century maps or working as an undertaker: find a way to tell the story of it in a way that would make someone else interested. The trick is to tease out that human strand that will engage the reader with your story.

EXERCISE 62

Flex your travel writing wings by starting from home, deliberately taking a trip by public transport to somewhere fairly local you've never been before. This might be a farmers' market, art gallery or local park. Be observant about the specifics and who you met along the way, finding original ways to describe what you've seen and felt about the experience. Keep the sense of exploration in mind.

EXERCISE 63

Put together a draft proposal for a non-fiction book on a subject of your choice. This should include a three-line pitch, and a three-page proposal including its market and *raison d'être*, with a chapter breakdown and outline.

EXERCISE 64

Make a note of everyday observations and ideas, perhaps in response to national and international news, as well as personal thoughts and feelings about them. This can help widen the scope of your thinking, which in turn can inform your non-fiction writing.

EXERCISE 65

Synonyms are words that have identical, close or similar meanings and it can be useful to substitute a word in your writing to avoid dull or repetitive text, or to create interesting images in the mind of a reader. Here, a *Roget's Thesaurus* is your friend. Find synonyms for the following words:

Love	Pungent	Discord	Abandon
Malevolent	Edge	Parsimonious	Oblique
Conundrum	Tedious	Burn	Sever

Things To Remember

- Whatever you want to write, factual writing helps develop voice, style and confidence.

- Have the courage of your convictions: there's no need to preface what you write with 'I think' as this is already implied.

- Accurate research underpins factual writing and fact checking is crucial ...

- ... it can also underpin fiction writing, too.

- Spell check everything unfamiliar, names in particular.

- Quotes in speech marks must be accurate: keep digital files for reference.

- If commissioned to write a piece, be sure you're clear on the brief (and agree a fee beforehand).

- Adjust your style for different forms: news writing should be objective, feature-writing can be more subjective.

09

Fiction

Fiction is the lie we give to truth, alleged Albert Camus, 20th-century French-Algerian philosopher, writer and Nobel prize-winning author of *L'Étranger* (*The Stranger*). And the first truth about fiction is that even if it's made up, it has to be *emotionally* truthful in order to be believable. If not truthful in its actual facts (with SciFi or fantasy fiction, for example) fiction must still be believable in the way the characters that deliver the story behave, think and speak. What happens to Alice in Wonderland might be fantastical, but her reactions to events are both realistic and in character.

At its heart, fiction is the essence of creative writing, because it's a sustained act of imagination about things a writer knows and imparts. Three key aspects to writing fiction are observation, experience and imagination. Use what's observed and experienced and apply imagination to it all. Fiction writers get to make up whole worlds, people and events and their skill lies in making these relatable in some way, even if the circumstances described are beyond our actual experience — and the writer's.

EXERCISE 66

Ideas

Sitting around waiting for inspiration won't work. It's always worth recording the germ of an idea, however fleeting, making notes, jotting it down and seeing what it might spark. This may involve some initial research about a subject or a person (definitely, if you want to write about an historical period) and it's in the process of exploration that storylines can be developed.

Often a story can develop from curiosity about something that strikes while the mind is off elsewhere, idling in neutral. How did X affect Y? What might it take for A to do B? What happened next? Literary creativity can be sparked by the literal 'What if ... ?' of an idea. Ideas often arise from trying to solve a problem. It's here that creative connectivity is a real friend and then, from a single proposition, whole books can be written.

Take a story that's really well known to you, something classic, perhaps like the children's story Goldilocks and the Three Bears. Subvert it. Turn it upside down and inside out, create characters and location and a whole different way to tell what is, essentially, the same story. Sketch out the bare bones of this in 500 words. Then, whatever story you've chosen to tell, restructure it from a different angle or in a different order. This helps create a sense of what it's possible to do with just the germ of an idea.

EXERCISE 67

Genre

Genre describes a particular style of fiction, and is often linked to the marketing of books, but it can be helpful to consider how fiction is categorised and into which literary category a piece of work might fall. Booksellers like to group books of similar categories together, even if there are subgenres within a genre, and this also makes it easier for readers to find what they're interested in.

Identify a book title that you know of for each of these categories, which will help you clarify which genre you are aiming for.

Romantic fiction
Science fiction
Fantasy
Crime or mystery fiction
Young adult fiction

Historical fiction
Literary fiction
Magic realism
Speculative fiction

EXERCISE 68

Take one emotion that is familiar to you and have it be experienced by a fictional character, describing how they might feel within an imagined set of circumstances. Keep it short, trying to show through their actions what they are feeling, and focussing on how that character expresses emotions (or not) in response to those specific circumstances.

EXERCISE 69

Show, don't tell

How do you know someone is feeling the way they are? Very few will explicitly say, 'I'm angry' or, 'I'm happy' but we know it from how they behave, and the more emotionally literate we are, the more easily we recognise the clues in people's behaviour and in what they say, or don't say. The same is true in writing. Instead of telling the reader how someone felt, in the examples below the woman's possible feelings towards the narrator are made clear through her actions.

- When she saw me, she smiled and skipped towards me.
- When she saw me, she scowled and stopped in her tracks.
- When she saw me, her eyes widened in fright and she ran.

Imagine a character who is unlike you in every way possible. Describe them, including examples of specific characteristics, and how these are expressed so that you show, rather than tell, what they are like.

EXERCISE 70

Details animate writing

One of the joys of writing is not only the writing itself, but also the exploration of what is being written about and may need researching. This could be the necessity for some major historical facts for an historical novel or a working knowledge of how to bake cakes for the character of a baker. The difference is that you're not writing a history book or a recipe book, so the knowledge is a working knowledge that provides an accurate backdrop that rings true. If there are wrong facts or anachronisms, these will jar and distract the reader in a way that makes them lose confidence in your writing.

Research and write about something that you don't already know about. For example, how to shear a sheep or travelling from one side of 18th-century Vienna to the other or the process of stitching a tapestry. Read details, look at pictures, watch clips, imagine the physicality of it. Write with attention to the detail that will bring your writing alive.

EXERCISE 71

Imagine your own day-to-day life, but in another era or set of circumstances: how would it remain similar, how would it differ? Be as precise as you can about the details, but as imaginative as you like about they might affect you.

EXERCISE 72

Take the word *fiction* and riff on the many variations of the word and how each of them can give you additional scope and ideas about what fiction might be, and how writing it could be approached.

Things To Remember

- Fiction is made up but it has to be rooted in what feels plausible to the plot and its characters.

- Curiosity is what makes imagination come alive. Harness both.

- Use personal experience, especially when it comes to writing about emotions, but keep them within your fictional characters' boundaries.

Prose

Any writing that isn't poetry is prose. Good prose is what sets a piece of writing apart, whether that's a novel, a newspaper article or even the instructions for a self-assembly chest of drawers. Clear in what it communicates, using words that are precise in their meaning, composed in well-constructed sentences, good prose is easy to read, its intent understood. If you have ever read a sentence and had to double back on it thinking, what is this writer actually saying?, then the prose is probably poor and not succeeding in communicating what the writer wants to say.

One of the benefits of reading well-written prose alongside your writing practice is that a lot of basic grammar skills get absorbed as if by osmosis. Then, through a regular practice of writing, it's possible to gain a working sense of the good sentence that is the basis of rigorous prose.

EXERCISE 73

In your writing, consciously experiment with sentence length and see how it contributes to the rhythm of a piece. Also, to its content. Short, staccato sentences can help convey fragmented information or thought processes. See how the form of a piece of writing can help convey its content.

EXERCISE 74

Practise getting your ideas into words by writing without stopping for 30 minutes. In this instance, ignore that self-censoring internal voice and forget the perfectly crafted sentence for the moment and just get it down ... all of it, in one fine creative muddle. This should yield about a thousand words. *Now* you have something to work with.

EXERCISE 75

Draft short descriptions (you can use metaphors and similes, too) to show what abstract concepts such as bravery, exhaustion, happiness and hunger might 'look' like through someone's actions or situation.

EXERCISE 76

Take a piece of past writing and edit and redraft it, tightening and refining it by omitting excess words. Sometimes this is just removing the 'padding', for example when we say something like, 'owing to the fact that' when we could say 'since' or 'because'.

EXERCISE 77

After the writing comes the revision. Taking a critical look at your own work is easier if you break it down. Does the structure work and provide a coherent storyline? Do your characters remain in character? Are the facts believable? And along the way, look for typos, grammatical errors and inconsistencies.

EXERCISE 78

Nouns and verbs: some words are both. For example, waffle, trot, poison, tweet and badger. When nouns are used as a verb, this is called *antimeria* and it can sometimes lift the language when you make unusual use of antimeria.

Make a list of 12 possibilities.

Things To Remember

- Prose is all writing that isn't poetry.

- Forget the perfect opening sentence: getting a first draft is your starting objective.

- Make the words you choose work hard: be specific and find the exact word you need.

- Frequent writing practice helps ground how you write and gives you confidence.

Poetry

The great American poet Elizabeth Bishop said that poetry was a way of 'thinking with one's feelings', while e e cummings, the American Modernist poet who threw away all constraints – grammar, syntax and form – in pursuit of a new way of writing dubbed *vers libre* (free verse), stated in one of his finest poems that 'feeling is first'. So if the inspiration for a poem comes primarily from a *feeling*, it is one that is crafted into some form of poetic narrative that expresses and describes that feeling in some way, whatever its form, whether it is a sonnet, haiku, villanelle or *vers libre*.

One of the benefits of writing poetry is that along with being a specific form of creative writing in its own right, it can also be a valuable exercise in learning how to specify and convey meaning in what you want to say irrespective of whether you want to write poetry. Playing with poetic forms is a way of exploring where your creative writing might take you and could function as an exploratory exercise that can enhance your writing skills generally.

EXERCISE 79

When starting a poem, it can be useful to make an initial list of words that might create a structural base for what you want to express. You could link these words by feeling or theme. Then, for each word, free associate and see what other words are sparked. Look for alternate meanings to the original word, and similar or discordant sounds. Keep your original aim firmly in mind but use this exercise to evoke some interesting associations that could be useful to your poem.

EXERCISE 80

Keeping a particular rhythm in mind – footsteps, heartbeat, drum beat – take a series of words to see how you can make them 'fit' through the stressed and unstressed syllables of the words. To get a sense of the rhythm, it always helps to read aloud what you've written. You may have to search for and substitute different words or word variations to achieve the rhythm you want.

EXERCISE 81

Compile a list of words that rhyme directly, and those that create a similar but not exact sound. For example: truth, youth, spoof, proof, wrath, cloth, sleep, feet, and so on. Sometimes the vowel sounds work together, as with 'ee' (assonance), or the consonants rhyme, as with 'th' (consonance).

EXERCISE 82

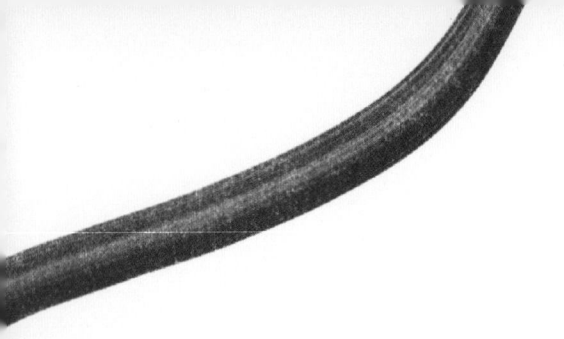

Write a poem using no punctuation at all. Free associate to get that first flow of feeling and then go back and see how you can combine a use of punctuation and line breaks to clarify what your poem is expressing.

EXERCISE 83

Whatever the theme of your poem, take its central idea and look at ways in which you can express it metaphorically. It doesn't matter how bizarre the link may seem initially, as long as you are clear on its points of connection. The idea is to create an evocation with which a reader can identify. For example, in Carol Ann Duffy's poem *Valentine* she uses the onion as a metaphor for love, which produces lots of unexpected ways in which they are both similar.

EXERCISE 84

Simile

Using a simile makes a comparison between two things that are often completely unrelated, designed to highlight one by its association with another using the words 'as' or 'like'. Poet Robert Burns used it when he said, 'My love is like a red, red rose', and William Wordsworth when he wrote 'I wandered lonely as a cloud'. Simile works to create a thought association in a way that's specific to the writer's intention.

Use similes. Describe someone's eyes as like … and don't go for the obvious, for example bright like diamonds or dull like muddy pools but find more interesting similes. If eyes don't appeal, try the moon; or something more abstract such as … footsteps. Whatever you choose, stick with it until you have come up with six ideas. You may never actually use these — some may be too subjective to work outside your own immediate frame of reference — but it's a way of practising creative connections that will help your writing.

EXERCISE 85

Idiom

An idiom is a phrase or saying that implies something different from its literal meaning. For example, referring to a 'perfect storm' isn't a reference to the weather but to the worst combination of events and outcome. Idioms occur in every language and don't always immediately translate because their literal meaning is different from their implied meaning.

Come up with new idioms to say the following:

- Everything is going wrong all at once.
- Move on, because the moment is past.
- In good health.
- Can't make up his mind.
- Get what you want by being nice.

Types of poetic form

Different poetic forms provide a structure within which you can explore some ideas. As an exercise, take a look at different examples and play with your own version of the same. There are accepted 'rules' to different poetic forms, but that doesn't mean you can't break them or mix them up as long as you comply with the idea of poetic rhythm.

EXERCISE 86

Sonnet
One of the oldest forms of poetry which consists of 14 lines, often broken down into three stanzas of four lines, completed with a rhyming couplet.

One way to get to grips with a sonnet is to start with the concluding two lines, the rhyming couplet, and then work backwards. This may seem counterintuitive, but it can help free up the creative mind if it knows where it's trying to end up.

EXERCISE 87

Haiku

The form for this depends on the number of syllables, rather than words. Haikus usually consist of up to 17 syllables arranged in three lines.

Take today's weather, whatever it is and wherever you are, and write a haiku.

EXERCISE 88

Villanelle

This consists of five stanzas of three lines and a final stanza of four lines. The last line of the first stanza is repeated in the third and the fifth stanzas; and the last line of the second stanza is repeated at the end of the fourth and sixth stanzas.

The villanelle is such a highly structured form it's a bit like a puzzle and, like a puzzle, starting from the outside and working in can sometimes help tackle it. Finding those repeating lines that encapsulate the theme, idea or feeling you want to express can be a good starting place for a villanelle.

EXERCISE 89

Epigram

An epigram doesn't always have to be a poem, but it does need to be a brief way in which an idea is expressed in a surprising or satirical manner.

Compose an epigram that celebrates hands – yours or someone else's – in some way, in four lines.

EXERCISE 90

Epitaph

Sometimes an epigram can also be an epitaph, when it pays tribute to someone, often in their memory after death and placed on a memorial or tombstone.

Write an epitaph to a goldfish, using six lines.

EXERCISE 91

Even if you are not subscribing to any poetic form, it's useful to set yourself some parameters. Start by making notes about the idea or feelings you want to express; gather together those words, phrases, references and themes you want to use; draft an initial sequence; edit, redraft, prune and discard as you clarify your thinking. Read it aloud to find the rhythm.

EXERCISE 92

Choose a favourite painting or picture and start by making a note of how it makes you *feel*; then note how you might express those feelings in direct response to it. You can include description of its content, form or colour. This is an ekphrastic poem and you can use any poetic form you wish for this.

EXERCISE 93

An acrostic poem takes each letter of the first line to form a word. Take any word, three lettered for a haiku, 14 lettered for a sonnet or any length you choose, and write a poem that relates to that word, using the 'rules' as above. Don't worry if it doesn't 'work', it's the connecting of words to ideas that you are exploring.

EXERCISE 94

Whatever feeling you're trying to express in your poem — nostalgia, anger, remorse, happiness, regret, longing, surprise — work with how those feelings might *sound* too and choose words that play on that to help extend their rhythmic usage.

Things To Remember

- Although there are no rules to writing poetry, there are general principles about what makes a poem.

- There must be a rhythm of sorts that runs through a poem.

- Rhyme isn't essential to a poem: the rhythm can come from other relationships between words, like alliteration or reiteration.

- Work with the relationship between the sounds and the sense of words: use them to create connections between ideas.

- Take time to incubate ideas; they sometimes take time to percolate through from the subconscious.

- Avoid all sentimentality and cliché, or at least subvert them: work towards something original and authentic to you. Be ruthless!

- Read poetry: read across different genres and styles and think about what draws you in, what makes a great poem, great; and what you could try emulating.

12

Memoir

What's the difference between memoir and autobiography? The distinction can become blurred but, generally speaking, a memoir is the telling of a life story by its subject based on their specific memories and the emotions they evoke, rather than a more factual, often linear, documentation of events, people, places from a more objective perspective.

Writing a memoir involves the same tools as writing anything else, including characterisation and dialogue, combining observation, experience and imagination to tell a story. This story is based on personal, lived experience, as it is remembered, and it is creatively realised in the writing using the same tools, in terms of voice and pace and how the narrative informs the structure of the story you're telling. You may start with your birth as the beginning of your life, or with some event in your life that was pivotal to its story, creating a nonlinear narrative to tell your story.

EXERCISE 95

Identify what for you is the pivotal event on which your memoir might rest. This pivotal event could be something to do with you, or to do with someone else, for example a parent's religious belief, or the birth of a sibling. It could be to do with a political shift or a geographical move to another place or country. This pivotal moment doesn't have to be historically significant, but it's useful to have a point of universal reference and also for it to be completely relevant to you. This can provide a useful focus to help you formulate the structure of a memoir. Write 500 words on what this is and then you have some material with which to work.

EXERCISE 96

Take a specific event in your life and focus on what you remember feeling, and how those feelings are relevant to what you remember. Try to be as specific as you can about the quality of those feelings. Take care over the adjectives or metaphors that you use to describe how you felt.

EXERCISE 97

Draft your personal back story in note form. This will help you evaluate key aspects that illuminate characteristics specific to you and relevant to the story you're telling, on which you can build.

EXERCISE 98

If you are writing dialogue as yourself, be true to yourself, flaws and all. Don't say things you wouldn't say in real life, otherwise it will jar. Real conversations range wide, with interruptions, pauses and repetitions, but in literature you need the bare bones of an exchange when committed to paper. This should add to, not repeat, some aspect of the story. Jot down highlights of an actual, remembered conversation and what might work as dialogue.

EXERCISE 99

Keep a daily note of memories, of colours, places, people, ideas, images that resonate back to childhood.

EXERCISE 100

Make a list of any words that are synonymous with, or aligned with, memory. This will help you think about what memory is, what purpose it plays, particularly in personal narratives, and what happens to memories over time.

Things To Remember

- Memory is inevitably subjective: it's your memory, your story and told from your subjective point of view.

- Memory is also unreliable, but the ambiguity of unreliable memory can be a relevant factor in a memoir.

- You have to take the reader on your personal journey, and the skill of your narrative is what will keep them interested.

- A writer's imagination extends into how a memoir is told and what tools are used in terms of chronology or structure, to make it come alive to a reader.

What Next?

Creative writing is something we can do for ourselves, as a way of thinking or organising our thoughts, keeping a record of our lives for ourselves or others, or just for fun. It is a way, as someone once said, of renovating the creative soul. It can help with everything from writing emails, academic essays or job applications to love letters or those of condolence. You may also feel you could write to be published and have been working towards this. You may even feel you now have something that's publishable. What's next?

There is no point approaching a non-fiction or academic publisher if you are looking to publish a novel. That much is obvious, but if you are interested in being published it is essential that you research who is publishing what.

- Start by browsing in bookshops and see who is publishing those books most akin to your own. See what publishing houses have imprints that relate well to what you're trying to do, whether it's fiction or non-fiction.

- When browsing recently published books to see who's published them, especially those that most closely resemble your own genre, check out the acknowledgements page. Often authors thank their agent, editor or publisher in person and that can give you a contact name.

- Take a look at the competition. See how similar or different your proposal might be.

- Search online for details of publishers' submission processes and discover if you need an agent to submit on your behalf.

- Don't submit whole manuscripts on spec as they probably won't get acknowledged, let alone read.

- This may all seem iniquitous when you *know* that you have written next year's bestseller, but it's also very hard to get published, so you may have to be as creative and tenacious in your research about where to pitch as in your writing to get there.

Things To Remember

- It sounds harsh but if you are writing to get published, then rejection will be part of that process and you're going to have to be utterly professional about this. Not only will you be rejected, but often you won't be given a reason, so don't expect to get your hand held, either.

- Explore other publishing venues and submit to magazines, online forums and competitions. Create a blog and social media profiles to platform your work and interact. If you can afford it, explore various workshops, attend events in bookshops and visit literary festivals to get a feel for the publishing industry.

Writer's Block

I include a note about this because I am asked about it all the time! While many will acknowledge that writer's block exists, few appear to agree what it is. Some say that writer's block is boredom, others that it's fear, but most professional writers expect some days to yield poor results and other days when the words seem to sing. That's fine. No professional writer expects to hone perfect sentences straight off. Yet all expect to write every day and are prepared to accept less than perfect work that they can craft. So they are never completely blocked. Trusting the process of writing itself, rather than expecting to produce immaculate work every time, helps lessen the fear. Acute fear, like depression and anxiety, can knock out cognitive function; the survival instincts of the primitive brain are privileged over the need to think things through. If those feelings arise, it can feel like there's a whole big blank. Ignore it and find some other way to come at it, for example:

- Write in your journal; write specifically about how you feel about anything and everything.

- Go for a walk, preferably in a park or somewhere that involves nature, to refresh your creative batteries.

- Read. Reading other people's work is never a waste of time.

- Cook, listen to music, visit an art gallery: do anything that might feed you creatively.

- Ponder life. Ideas percolate all the time. Sit in contemplation; write them down.

- Take one small scene from the middle of what you want to write and write it up. Repeat until you are littered with small scenes which you can work and rework. You are creating the fabric of your writing.

Further Reading

Aspects of the Novel, E.M. Forster, Penguin Classics

Creative Journal Writing, Stephanie Dowrick, Tarcher Penguin

How Fiction Works, James Wood, Vintage

How Not to Write a Novel, Sandra Newman & Howard Mittelmark, Penguin

How To Write Well, Tim de Lisle, Connell Guides

Into the Woods: How stories work and why we tell them, John Yorke, Penguin

Letters to a Young Writer, Colum McCann, Bloomsbury

How to Grow Your Own Poem, Kate Clanchy, Swift Press

On Writing, Stephen King, Hodder

The Anatomy of Story, John Truby, Faber & Faber

The Artist's Way, Julia Cameron, Macmillan

The Creative Writing Course Book, eds. Julia Bell & Paul Magrs, Macmillan

The Elements of Style, William Strunk Jr & E.B. White, Pearson Education

The Five-Minute Writer, Margret Geraghty, How To Books

The Poem, Don Patterson, Faber & Faber

The Right to Write, Julia Cameron, Hay House

What If? Anne Bernays & Pamela Painter, Collins

Your Story: How to write it so others will want to read it, Joanne Fedler, Hay House

Websites

creativewritingconsultancy.co.uk

literaryconsultancy.co.uk

literarydevices.net

merriam-webster.com

nationalcentreforwriting.org.uk

poetryfoundation.org

poetryschool.com

writers-online.co.uk

writersandartists.co.uk

writerscircle.com

writersdigest.com

writersretreats.org

About The Author

Harriet Griffey has an MA in Modern and Contemporary Literature and is a tutor at the Creative Writing Consultancy. She also facilitates writers' retreats at writersretreats.org and was previously a commissioning editor at George Allen & Unwin and editorial director at Macdonald Publishers. Author of over 40 books, she has been published not only by Hardie Grant but also by Penguin, Bloomsbury and Pan Macmillan. As a journalist she has previously written for all the UK national newspapers and elsewhere, was a book reviewer for the *Financial Times* and cultural editor for *The Ecologist*.

Acknowledgements

Thanks are due, as ever, to my lovely team of collaborators at Hardie Grant, but particularly Isabel Gonzalez-Prendergast and Chelsea Edwards for overseeing this new edition.

And also, last but never least, my own children Josh and Robbie, whose existence is its own creative inspiration.

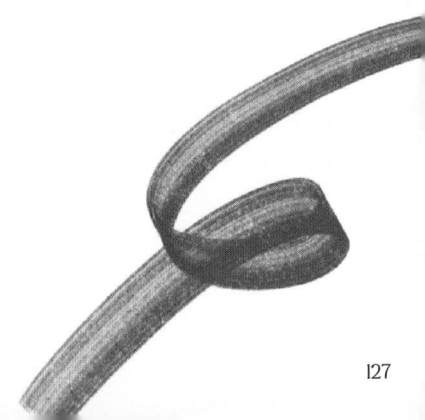

Published in 2024 by Hardie Grant Books (London)

Hardie Grant Books (London)
5th & 6th Floors
52–54 Southwark Street
London SE1 1UN

hardiegrantbooks.com

All rights reserved. No part of this
publication may be reproduced, stored in
a retrieval system or transmitted in any
form by any means, electronic, mechanical,
photocopying, recording or otherwise,
without the prior written permission of
the publishers and copyright holders.
The moral rights of the author
have been asserted.

Copyright text © Harriet Griffey 2024

British Library Cataloguing-in-Publication Data.
A catalogue record for this book is
available from the British Library.

Write Now
ISBN: 9781784887674

10 9 8 7 6 5 4 3 2 1

Publishing Director: Kajal Mistry
Commissioning Editor: Isabel Gonzalez-Prendergast
Senior Project Editor: Chelsea Edwards
Design: Hannah Valentine
Proofreader: Clare Double
Production Controller: Gary Hayes

Colour reproduction by p2d
Printed and bound in China by
RR Donnelley Asia Printing Solution Limited

MIX
Paper | Supporting
responsible forestry
FSC® C018179